the little book of trikes

adam quellin

T0386791

Also from Veloce –

BMW Boxer Twins 1970-1995 Bible, The (Falloon)
BMW Custom Motorcycles – Choppers, Cruisers, Bobbers, Trikes & Quads (Cloesen)
Ducati 750 Bible, The (Falloon)
Ducati 750 SS 'round-case' 1974, The Book of the (Falloon)
Ducati 860, 900 and Mille Bible, The (Falloon)
Ducati Monster Bible, The (Falloon)
Funky Mopeds (Skelton)

Italian Custom Motorcycles (Cloesen)
Kawasaki Triples Bible, The (Walker)
Lambretta Bible, The (Davies)
little book of smart, the New Edition (Jackson)
little book of microcars, the (Quellin)
Microcars at Large! (Quellin)
Moto Guzzi Sport & Le Mans Bible, The (Falloon)
Motorcycle Road & Racing Chassis Designs (Noakes)
Scooters & Microcars, The A-Z of Popular (Dan)

www.veloce.co.uk

First published in September 2011 by Veloce Publishing Limited, Veloce House, Parkway Farm Business Park, Middle Farm Way, Poundbury, Dorchester, Dorset, DT1 3AR, England.
Fax 01305 250479/e-mail info@veloce.co.uk/web www.veloce.co.uk or www.velocebooks.com.

ISBN: 978-1-845842-95-6 UPC: 6-36847-04295-0

Readers with ideas for automotive books, or books on other transport or related hobby subjects, are invited to write to the editorial director of Veloce Publishing at the above address.
British Library Cataloguing in Publication Data – A catalogue record for this book is available from the British Library.
Typesetting, design and page make-up all by Veloce Publishing Ltd on Apple Mac.
Printed in India by Imprint Digital.

VELOCE PUBLISHING
THE PUBLISHER OF FINE AUTOMOTIVE BOOKS

contents

introduction &
acknowledgements

introduction

The machines featured in this book are three-wheeled vehicles of motorcycle origin. Some have bike engines, some car engines, but nearly all have motorcycle front forks, with a single front wheel and two at the rear. There are one or two exceptions to this. The classic Morgan three-wheeled sports car has two front wheels and one rear, but has its roots in motorcycling, especially with its engines. Trikes are an individual, fun, and even practical means of transport. A tight turning circle and excellent visibility will allow you to fill the smallest gaps or motorcycle parking bays. Trikes offer an open road experience like a motorcycle, with similar power to match. People wary of motorcycles often make willing passengers on a trike, too. It is widely believed that a vehicle with a single front wheel is inherently unstable and likely to tip over at the slightest provocation. With a low centre of gravity, ride height, and wide rear track, this doesn't have to be so. Despite their obvious bulk, many of the Honda Goldwing derived trikes have excellent roadholding capabilities, and are surprisingly nimble in traffic.

Trikes also offer an alternative for the disabled motorcycle enthusiast. They can be the perfect antidote for those forced to retire from motorcycling due to accident or illness. A spell in the saddle of a trike could be just the tonic for those who are coming to terms with a disability, and can no longer ride a conventional motorcycle. In the UK, a charity called the National Association for Bikers with a Disability exists to promote motorcycling for the disabled, offers advice, and even organises triking events.

Trikes, and most cars with three wheels, enjoy certain tax concessions in the UK and parts of Europe. They can be ridden or driven by holders of a full car or full motorcycle licence. Vehicles you sit on and straddle

Many of today's trikers are disabled riders.

like a motorcycle don't require seat belts. The Directive for European Whole Vehicle Approval of two- and three-wheeled vehicles refers to a motor tricycle as having three symmetrically arranged wheels. This rules out motorcycle and sidecar combinations.

Trikes have been around since the dawn of motoring. The first self-propelled car, in 1769, was a three-wheeler, and the first internal combustion-engined car, in 1896, also had three wheels. Piaggio first introduced its own trike, based on its successful Vespa scooters, back in 1948. In 1933, Raleigh was producing a three-wheeled delivery van, powered by a 750cc V-twin engine. Reliant went on to build a similar version in 1935. These were, of course, all utility vehicles, built with a practical purpose. In later years, trikes have enjoyed increasing popularity, especially in the United States, where warm weather and long straight roads inspire a sense of freedom and adventure. This book explores some of the trikes around today, both the one-offs and the mass-produced. It also takes a backward glance at some of the trikes which have influenced them.

acknowlegements

I would like to thank the following people for their help with this book:

Andy at LIA Imports, Paul Richards at QB Motorcycles, Maria at Rewaco Trikes and the Rewaco Owners' Club, Ann Fisher and Kent Wings Goldwing Owners' Club, Big Al of Budget Trikes, Barry Walton at Colin Appleyard, Mark Grinnall of Grinnall Specialist Cars, Matt Bullock and James Bushell of 158 Performance, Simon Bell Design, Bill Hill of Commuter Concepts, Damien Kimberley of the Coventry Transport Museum, Malcolm Bull, Geordie, Joe 90 of Eagles MCC, Brothers of the Third Wheel, Pete Collins, Simon Farrier, Graham Shaw, Elvis Payne, Skunk, Rat, Phil Waiton, Grum, Foggy, Ged Kettle, anyone else whose trike appears in these pages, all at Veloce for allowing me a second bite at the cherry, and for my understanding wife, Carol, who saw so little of me during the long hours spent working on the little book you have in your hands.

chapter 1

early trikes

One trike which seems to have been widely copied is the Harley-Davidson Servi-Car. In order to boost flagging sales during the Great Depression, Harley-Davidson introduced the Servi-car in 1932. Intended as a vehicle to be towed behind a garage customer's car, the Servi-Car could be conveniently ridden back to the garage after delivery. It soon became a handy vehicle for delivery people, small vendors, and even some police departments.

In Europe, Piaggio introduced its successful range of tiny delivery vans and pick-ups, based on the popular Vespa scooters. It was called the 'Ape,' pronounced 'ah-pay,' meaning 'bee' in Italian. The little Ape began in 1947, and came with a choice of 50cc, 125cc, and 150cc engines. A 175cc option came later. It was often referred to as the VespaCar or TriVespa, and came in numerous different body styles. The Ape had a single front wheel, with handlebars and controls akin to a scooter. It remains in production to this day.

Although more of a car with three wheels than a three-wheeled motorcycle, it is still worth mentioning the legendary Morgan. Company founder HFS Morgan decided to build himself a trike back in 1909, using a Peugeot twin-cylinder 7hp engine. He called it the Morgan Runabout, and it attracted favourable attention. He decided to make a few more and obtained his first design patent in 1910. The following year, two Runabouts were exhibited at Olympia, fitted with JAP 8hp twin and 4hp single-cylinder engines. Morgan's little three wheelers were successful in trials and races, and by 1913, his company was producing racing cars. Early cars were single seaters, with tiller steering. In 1931, a model with three speeds, and reverse with chain drive to the single rear wheel, was introduced. Morgan switched to car engines in 1935, and stopped making three wheelers in 1952, to concentrate on the four-wheeled sports cars.

Harley Davidson's Servi-Car could be towed behind a car, and then driven back to the garage. It was a handy tool for dealerships delivering cars to customers. First available in 1932, it enjoyed a long production life with several changes made along the way. It was originally offered with a single drum brake at the rear. By 1937, however, operators enjoyed the sophistication of drum brakes on each wheel. Reverse gear was fitted from 1933.

It was powered initially by a 45in³ flat-head (side-valve) engine, as fitted to the 'R' type motorcycle of the time. In 1937, the Servi-Car was fitted with the same engine as the 'W' type motorcycle, which had a more efficient method of lubrication. The vehicle had a rear track of 1100mm (42in), and was made wide enough to follow in the tracks of cars of the era on unpaved roads.

The Piaggio Ape, pronounced 'ah-pay,' was a three-wheeled version of the iconic Vespa scooter. The Vespa first grew its third wheel in 1947, and had a wooden pick-up load area. It was powered by a 125cc engine, and featured a column-mounted gear lever. However, by 1956, the Ape had an enclosed cab, and the option of electric start. Numerous changes occurred throughout its production life, and a wide range of engines was available. Early models had the engine lurking under the front seat, but it was later moved to the rear to cut out some of the noise and fumes. To date, the smallest Ape has a 50cc two-stroke engine, and the largest one, a 422cc Lombardini diesel unit. The compact size of this vehicle makes it very manoeuvrable and easy to park in city streets. It is also built under licence in India by Bajaj, and is a common sight plying its trade as an autorickshaw, or tuk-tuk. The name 'tuk-tuk' was given to these vehicles due to the sound of the engine. Pictured here is a Bajaj autorickshaw, imported into the UK by The Tukshop.

Back in 1909, the first Morgan was a single seater runabout three-wheeler, built by HFS Morgan for his own needs. However, it attracted much attention, so Morgan decided to build a few more, and so set up his own manufacturing business. Realising the potential of a two-seater, he expanded his workshops and purchased additional machining tools. Morgans were known as cyclecars at the time, due to their lightweight construction. They entered races and hill climbs with great success, and one Morgan vehicle won the Cyclecar Grand Prix, driven by WG McMinnies. McMinnies was editor of *Cyclecar* magazine at the time. This model then became known as the Grand Prix. Early Morgans had two speeds, and two rear chains providing the drive to the single rear wheel. By 1931, these machines had three speeds and reverse, with just a single chain coming from a bevel box behind the gearbox, and then on to the rear sprocket. The vehicle pictured here is a 1933 Morgan Super Sports, fitted with a Matchless V-twin air-cooled engine. Entry is by stepping over the body tub. The Morgan Motor Company stopped producing three-wheelers in 1952 to concentrate on building its four-wheelers. Today, the Morgan Motor Company eschews modern production line assembly methods for hand-built techniques. The style of the three-wheeled Morgan has been widely copied. Several kit car manufacturers have built their own version, fitted with Citroën 2CV or V-twin motorcycle engines.

Pictured here is a Triking, designed and built by former Lotus employee Tony Divey. Inspired by the original Morgan, this kit car is powered by a Moto Guzzi engine.

In 1934, Chief Designer for Raleigh's Motor Department, Tom Williams left the company to start his own business producing three wheelers. Ably assisted by former Raleigh repair shop foreman ES Thompson, Williams built a prototype powered by a JAP 600cc single-cylinder air-cooled engine. Chain drive, handlebar steering, and a central driving position were used. However, a steering wheel was used on production models. The whole vehicle was then clothed in an aluminium van body with a wooden frame. The first production Reliant 7cwt 'girder-fork' van was delivered in June 1935. A larger van, called the 10cwt, was similar to the previous model, but had the driver seated to the right, more like a car. Drive to the rear wheels was now by shaft, and the single-cylinder engine was replaced by a water-cooled JAP V-twin engine of 747cc. As time progressed, Reliant used side-valve Austin

Seven engines, until 1939, when the Austin engine was no longer available. The company then produced its own engines, based on the Austin unit. By the 1950s, Reliant was moving into the passenger car market, and eventually came up with the Regal. Early Regals had aluminium bodywork, but by 1956, were made in fibreglass. Reliant went on to produce a more refined overhead valve engine. In 1973, the Regal was replaced by the Robin. Although the subject of much derision, the Robin's 750cc and 850cc all-alloy engine was an economical and sprightly performer. It is still a popular choice for trike builders today.

This is possibly the oldest Reliant vehicle in existence. Based on the Raleigh LDV van, designer Tom Williams left the Raleigh company to produce his own three-wheeled vans. Power was via a JAP single-cylinder, air-cooled engine, developing 8hp. This engine was linked to a Burman three-speed and reverse gearbox with a chain. Another duplex chain drove the rear axle. (Courtesy Elvis Payne)

The Triumph Tina Trike was based on the Triumph Tina scooter, and was designed by George Wallis, the man who had worked on the BSA Ariel Three, a three-wheeled leaning moped. The Triumph Tina scooter was powered by a 100cc automatic V-belt drive two-stroke engine. The two rear wheels were driven via a differential. Twelve prototypes were built, but failed negotiations with BSA ensured the trike never entered mass production. Wallis then approached car manufacturer Daihatsu. Daihatsu developed its own little trike, which used Wallis' engineering principles. It was called the Daihatsu Hallo, but was never sold in the UK. It seems a shame that the tilting delivery trike has not been successful outside of Japan, as it would be a practical form of transport for the small business. Top speed of the Tina Trike was 40mph (65km/h), and it had a rear track of 30in (762mm).
(Courtesy Coventry Transport Museum)

This little moped trike was the creation of George Wallis, and was introduced around 1970. Known as the BSA Ariel Three, it was unusual at the time because it had a system which allowed the front part of the machine to pivot, while the rear remained level. This allowed the little trike to lean round corners like a conventional motorcycle. Riding on skinny 12in pressed steel wheels, and featuring a white plastic fairing, it had a flimsy look about it. The tilting mechanism also employed two torsion rods, which allowed the rear wheels to steer a tighter turn. With correct adjustment, cornering was a smooth, progressive occasion, but many riders experienced panic, as slack in the rods was taken up, and the machine turned more sharply than they had anticipated.

The Ariel Three had a 50cc fan-cooled, single-cylinder, two-stroke engine, made by the Dutch Anker company. There was no differential, instead, the nearside rear wheel was driven by chain and sprocket. A toothed belt was also connected to the clutch pulley. A fan mounted outboard of the engine drive pulley often resulted in overheating, unless the vehicle was moving. A Bosch flywheel magneto provided lighting power, although the trike was never fitted with a rear brake light. The 50cc engine produced 1.7bhp (kW) at 5500rpm. The main frame was a steel pressing, and the plastic front mudguard and engine side covers did little to exude a feeling of quality. It was an unreliable machine, and its development contributed to the financial downfall of BSA. Only a few hundred were built, and production ceased in mid-1971. However, the tilting idea was a useful one, and attracted the attention of the Japanese. Honda finally took the prototypes and designs back to Japan, but it wasn't until several years later, in 1984, that Honda marketed the Gyro. The Gyro is still in production today, but not readily available outside Japan. Tilting trike fans outside the Land of the Rising Sun will have to settle for China's offering – the Xingyue Vogue.
(Courtesy Coventry Transport Museum)

professional trike builders

The Dutch sidecar manufacturer and engineering company EML was founded by Hennie Winkelhuis in 1972. The firm first converted motorcycles into trikes in 1999. The first trike was based on a Honda Goldwing GL 1500, and created "quite a storm," according to the motorcycling press at the time. Known as the 'Bermuda,' this trike featured disc brakes all round, leading link front suspension forks, and a car type front wheel. This took place at the factory in Neede in the Netherlands. Winkelhuis later sold this part of the business

The Dutch motorcycle frame and sidecar manufacturer EML first built trikes in 1999. Its first machine was based on the Honda Goldwing GL 1500. The EML Martinique pictured here at the Colin Appleyard showroom in Keighley, West Yorkshire, UK, is based on the Goldwing 1800. It has the option of the ExtensoDive fork set. The manufacturer claims that the ExtensoDive fork provides a greater level of comfort than the common swing arm, without compromising stability and road holding. A strengthened steering head and forks, which use solid tubes and external springs bolted to the front of them, are the order of the day. This feature first appeared on the Bermuda model. The Martinique GT appears to be large and unwieldy, but is no wider than a small car at 1380mm (54.3in). Overall length is 2780mm (109.4in) and the wheelbase is 1790mm (70.4in). This top-of-the-range trike has very practical stowage space, too. The luggage compartment is 145 litres in capacity (5.1ft³), so there is plenty of scope for long distance touring. This machine is also fitted with an electric reverse gear, although it always pays to be selective about where you park, as with any trike or large motorcycle. The donor motorcycle uses an 1800cc six-cylinder, horizontally-opposed, liquid-cooled engine. Maximum power output is 117bhp at 5500rpm.

to concentrate on building quad bikes. Sadly, Winkelhuis died in 2001, but the company still thrives, producing road bikes, sidecars, and trikes. Importantly, EML builds trike kits, which are supplied to dealers, such as Colin Appleyard in the UK. Trike conversion kits are not sold to the general public, but to dealers, who then sell the finished product. The Martinique kit converts a Honda Goldwing 1800 motorcycle to a trike, and is currently the market leader. A GT model has recently been released, with a wider body. The Bermuda kit uses a 1500 Goldwing base bike for its trike conversion. Aluminium MOMO design rear wheels are standard feature. A 14in front wheel, chrome rear brace, lockable parking brake, stainless brake hoses, and stainless steel exhausts add to the feel of quality. Honda's six-cylinder boxer engine will whisk this trike up to 170km/h, and will consume fuel at a rate of one litre for every 10km (28mpg UK or 23.5mpg US).

The first Lehman trike was completed in 1984. A 1981 Honda CB 900 was the donor bike John Lehman used. Built for his own use, in his garage, the trike attracted attention from others. It also aroused a general interest in this type of vehicle. This was traded in for another conventional motorcycle, but the following year, a second trike was built using a 1984 Honda GL 1200 Goldwing. It was originally fitted with a wooden body, but then replaced with a fibreglass shell. It was again sold, and Lehman himself then realised the commercial potential. Lehman Trikes began in Westlock, Alberta, in Canada, and is currently based in Spearfish, South Dakota in the US. The first Harley-Davidson conversion was completed in 1991. Since then, Lehman has also carried out trike conversions on BMW, Suzuki, and Victory motorcycles. By 2000, Lehman Trikes was enjoying an enthusiastic following, and an owners' club was established, called 'Lehman Pride.' This also coincided with the manufacturer's 15th anniversary.

Matt Wright served his apprenticeship with a company who produced steam turbines and gas compressors for marine and electric

Pictured here is an EML machine, mid-way through its transformation from bike to trike. The conversion is taking place at Colin Appleyard's trike centre in Yorkshire, UK. EML doesn't sell kits to customers, but supplies them to trike dealers, who then carry out the conversions. It is quite a complex process, not merely a simple matter of bolting an axle onto a bike frame. As can be seen here, the donor bike has been stripped down to a skeleton, and the trike frame carefully grafted into place. Rear disc brakes and axle are from a Mercedes. It is unlikely the popular Reliant axle would be robust enough to transmit the power to the rear wheels.

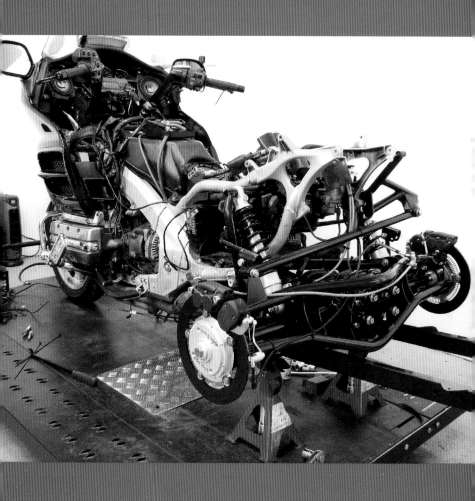

This very tidy looking trike was photographed at the 'Brightona' bike and trike custom show, an annual event for biking and triking enthusiasts in Brighton, on the south coast of England. This Honda Goldwing trike is the ultimate in luxury trike travel. The 1800cc horizontally-opposed, six-cylinder engine is smooth and powerful, and capable of swallowing up thousands of miles with ease. A vertical lift boot/trunk hatch allows easy access for loading. Sumptuous leather seats, with a backrest for the passenger, ensure this trike is a comfortable place to be. Riders are further cosseted by isolastic cushion ride suspension.

Another example of the popular Goldwing-based trike. This machine has single-piece rear bodywork, similar to Lehman and EML trikes.

generation industries. He then worked as a coded welder, and also spent ten years in the kit car industry. A passion for bike to trike conversions inspired him to set up his own business, and Casarva Custom Conversions was born in 2005. Based in Peterborough, UK, Casarva will convert customer's bikes to trikes, and will supply its own kit to those who wish to carry out the work themselves. The company will even supply a turn-key trike.

This is one of Casarva Trike's conversions, based on the Honda Valkyrie. The Valkyrie was made from 1997 to 2003, and used the same 1520cc (93in³) water-cooled, horizontally-opposed, flat-six engine as the Goldwing model. Note the six open-mouth carburettors. By way of contrast, later Goldwings use fuel injection. Transmission is a five-speed, with shaft drive to the rear wheels, via a Ford Sierra differential. The differential is mounted in a cradle, with fabricated wishbones top and bottom. There is plenty of chrome to keep its proud owner busy. Casarva can supply kits for shaft drive, chain or belt drive bikes, with the further option of a wide or narrow rear track, 1530mm (60in) and 1300mm (51in) respectively. On vehicles with the narrow rear track, the Ford drive shafts would need to be shortened. (Courtesy Simon Bell Design)

The finish on this Yamaha based trike is particularly fine. The suspension setup is the same as the Honda Valkyrie trike – a tried and tested formula of independent rear suspension, with unequal length wishbones and coilover shock absorber springs. Note also the marker lamps on the rear mudguards. These forward facing sidelamps are fitted to comply with lighting regulations in the UK, and to provide oncoming traffic with an indication of width. (Courtesy Simon Bell Design)

Detail of the independent rear suspension can be seen here on this Yamaha-based trike. The engineering is of a very high standard, and all the components have been powder coated for a durable finish. Provision is made for camber adjustment on the top suspension wishbone. The chrome tubing and rear lamp mounting brackets are elegantly made. (Courtesy Simon Bell Design)

This is the kit Casarva offers to customers, prior to powder coating. The kit shown is for bikes with a belt drive system, as can be seen by the teeth on the external crownwheel. Parts offered to carry out the conversion include: suspension wishbones, camber adjusters, hub carriers, cycle wing brackets, poly bushes, insert tubes, and a bolt kit. A differential is also supplied with the belt and chain drive kits. Owners of shaft drive bikes need to supply a differential from a Ford Sierra car. (Courtesy Simon Bell Design)

This elegant-looking Harley-Davidson trike in black and white livery has a low seat, which must make it very relaxing for cruising.

Grinnall Specialist Cars

Grinnall Specialist Cars has produced some very striking designs at its workshops in Bewdley, Worcestershire, UK. It currently produces the Scorpion-III, the Scorpion-IV, the R3T trike, and the BMW R1200C, CL, and R1150R trikes. Grinnall has plans to launch

The Grinnall Scorpion-III was first produced in 1992. Steve Harper, an accomplished designer for a company called Shado, designed the bodywork. Mark Grinnall and Neil Williams designed the chassis and chose the BMW 'K' series motorcycle engine as the power unit. This engine is a water cooled four-cylinder type, and comes in various capacities: 1100cc, 1200cc, and 1300cc. Power output ranges from 100bhp to 180bhp. Early 1100 and 1200cc Scorpions used a car-type single-plate dry clutch, but the later 1300cc engine has a wet oil-bath multi-plate clutch. This engine is found in the K40 series BMW motorcycle. The early 1100 Scorpion has a five-speed gearbox; 1200cc and 1300cc versions have six speeds. An electric reverse is available on some versions. The Scorpion, also known as the S-III, uses the same rear suspension setup as the BMW motorcycle, with a swinging arm and 'para-lever' system. This helps prevent the vehicle rising up under hard acceleration. Driver and passenger sit on orthopaedically-designed seats. The vehicle weighs a mere 390kg (858lb), so an impressive power to weight ratio is guaranteed. (Courtesy Mark Grinnall/Grinnall Specialist Cars)

the latest in its growing range of trikes; one is based on the sensational Triumph Thunderbird 1600. The company earned itself a good reputation by successfully modifying Triumph TR7 and TR8 sportscars. Even the Triumph Register recognised the Grinnall Triumph TR7 as a marque in its own right, thus earning the company an excellent reputation. In 1991, Mark Grinnall, a keen motorcycling enthusiast, set to work developing a trike, with two front wheels and one rear. The aim was to produce something more technically advanced than previous three-wheeled designs. In 1992, the S-III was introduced, and has become well regarded on the kit car scene. Following on from the success of the S-III, Grinnall began developing the S-IV, a four-wheeler. In 1999, work began on the first of Grinnall's motorcycle derived trikes, with two rear wheels and one front. The donor bike was the BMW R1200C – a machine that had the twin advantages of BMW's tele-lever front suspension and shaft drive. Launched in 2000, this trike has been a constant seller for Grinnall. Following in the BMW trike's success, a new model was launched, based on the Triumph Rocket.

Grinnall's first motorcycle trike was the BMW 1150R Trike which debuted in 2000. Next trike on the scene was the R3T, based on the Triumph Rocket, as shown here. It has a 2300cc fuel-injected, three-cylinder, in-line engine. Its large capacity and massive torque allow a breathtaking 0-100mph (160 km/h) in around 10 seconds. Top speed is over 120mph. A sturdy rear frame is bolted to the original bike frame. It is mounted at the swinging arm, lower engine mountings, rear upper frame, and shock absorber mounting points. Like the BMW trike, it also has independent double wishbone rear suspension and adjustable shock absorbers. Additionally, it has an inboard anti-roll bar. CNC aluminium billet double-clamp fork yokes ensure a reduced trail, and therefore, low cornering effort. There is also the electric reverse. The reversing gearwheel acts as a brake disc, and a mechanical calliper squeezes against it as the handbrake is operated. A similar system is used on the BMW. Rear wheels are bespoke billet items, and are shod with 225/45/17 Toyo tyres. Like the BMW trike, the R3T converts a Triumph supplied directly from the manufacturer. However, customers can purchase a kit from Grinnall to carry out the work themselves. This includes body panels, as well as the usual suspension and axle components. Build time is around 80 hours.
(Courtesy Mark Grinnall/Grinnall Specialist Cars)

Budget Trikes

Alan Cayliss, often known as 'Big Al,' has been building trikes since 1969. His company, Budget Trikes, is based in Lincolnshire, UK. Budget Trikes is a small operation, with Big Al doing the trike conversions, and his assistant 'Cuff' helping out and running the errands. Budget Trikes has produced a rich and varied selection of trikes over the years. Big Al's forty years of experience is clearly shown in the level of craftsmanship and engineering skill involved in each trike. A customer's bike can be 'triked.' Big Al also sells complete turn-key trikes. His company does not, however, sell kits. One option for a conversion is to use the existing swing arm of the donor bike to take the rear axle required. A bespoke independent rear suspension can be fabricated to accept a Ford Sierra final drive unit. Reliant rear axles can be shortened, if necessary, to create a narrower rear track. A trike rear axle can be bolted onto the swing arm and attached to the donor bike's shock absorbers, in a conversion frame. Alternatively, the system can be welded onto the bike. However, if this more permanent method is used, the trike would subsequently be subject to rigorous Motorcycle Single Vehicle Approval (MSVA) testing. A bolt-on system is generally viewed as an accessory, which means the motorcycle can be returned to its original specification. In this case, the machine is simply inspected by the local Driver and Vehicle Licencing Authority, to confirm its identity. Each project throws up its own challenges, but Big Al remembers some problems encountered when building a BMW K1200 based trike. The answer was to fabricate a new subframe for the axle to be mounted safely. Building a trike with independent suspension is more time consuming and costly than one with a rigid axle, but it is all a matter of customer preference. Many trikes Budget Trikes produce are Reliant based, although the most popular ones are the bike-based models. Big Al reckons the Yamaha Virago, Suzuki Intruder, and Honda CX 500 are good donor bikes.

Big Al, proprietor of Budget Trikes, with a Reliant-based trike part way through the build.

Side view showing the shape of the frame. Budget Trikes is one of many businesses which can convert a bike to trike for the customer. This particular frame is bespoke.

Here is the completed trike. It was built from scratch, and is now ready to be sold. The curved mudguards and pinstripe detailing add a touch of style. The stepped seat provides the rider with comfort on long journeys. All the ancilliaries and wiring are neatly fitted, with nothing hanging loose or looking cluttered. The prop shaft has been shortened. Note also the gusset plates welded in near the handbrake lever, and behind the headstock, to provide extra frame rigidity. (Courtesy Big Al at Budget Trikes)

This Suzuki Intruder would have been a fairly straightforward trike conversion. The rear axle on this trike is from a Reliant car, and is bolted to coil-over shock absorbers that are also attached to the frame of the trike. A swinging arm each side of the axle is fitted in place of the original chain stays. This setup is often referred to as a 'hard tail.' Also note the cable running from the left handlebar to an actuating mechanism by the gear lever. This is to allow a twist grip gear change operation.

Ann Fisher is a member of the Kent Wings Goldwing Trike Owners' Club. She bought her Motortrike second-hand from a disabled biker. She calls it 'Spirit of Dreams,' which summarises her passion for trikes. Ann bought the trike as she can ride it on a car licence, unlike a two-wheeled bike, and she'll find any excuse to be out and about on her trike. She has ridden it across Spain, Luxemburg, Italy, and Scotland. Despite its size, she asserts it is easy to park, thanks to an excellent turning circle, and it's fine in traffic. She even uses it to nip to the shops sometimes. The Motortrike is made in Texas, and uses a Ford Ranger rear axle. This axle is also found in the six-cylinder Ford Mustang. The Motortrike also has that extremely useful reverse gear. In addition, Motortrike produces a Harley-Davidson version called the 'Trog.'

The Honda CX 500 is a good trike donor. The 500cc liquid-cooled twin-cylinder engine is smooth and reliable, and the bike frame is conventional enough to have its rear end adapted. Another plus point is the visual appeal of the engine, with a large cylinder protruding each side of the fuel tank.

The Yamaha Virago forms a good basis for a trike, due to its conventional frame layout. Its seating layout also makes it very comfortable. It was the first Japanese V-twin cruiser style motorcycle. Originally fitted with mono-shock rear suspension, it was later given a dual-shock system. It was made from 1981, up until 2007. A variety of engine sizes were available from 125cc, right up to 1100cc. The first Virago was a 750cc, and the last one to be made was a 250cc.

This is the Arrowhead trike, built by Eurotech Trikes in Colliers Green, Kent, UK. To drive it, the operator kneels in it and adopts a rather head-first, racing position. It is constructed from a space frame chassis, and clothed in a lightweight fibreglass body. Steering is handlebar type, Formula 2 sidecar style. It has independent rear suspension, with elliptical wishbones, pivoting arms, and race shock absorbers. The power unit is a Yamaha 1200 Legend race car engine. It just proves what a vast array of trike designs there are. The only constraints are budget and the trike builder's imagination. Eurotech will convert any bike to a trike, whether it's a scooter or a cruiser. It can also convert a bike to a two front-wheel configuration, as well as the usual two rear-wheel layout.

Trike Design, incorporating Hank's Chop Shop, carries out all types of engineering work; chopper building, custom work, and adaptations, as well as trikes. Hank and Robin have been working together for twenty five years, and this Harley-Davidson-derived trike is their latest venture. Called the Brooklands, it has a modular type of rear bodywork. The main body is moulded separately to the mudguards, which is an advantage if any part should get damaged, as there is no need to replace the whole body. There is also the flexibility of changing the mudguards to suit different types of wheel. The compact nature of the independent rear suspension also allows greater luggage space.

Comprehensive instrumentation of the Brooklands Trike.

Axe Customs carried out the conversion to Graham Shaw's Suzuki Bandit 1200. Graham already had a Suzuki GS 850 trike, which he was delighted with, but wanted another trike with independent rear suspension. His GS 850 has a 'hard tail,' a solid axle from a Reliant. Graham says his Bandit trike is smooth, powerful, and easy to ride. There are no steering wobbles, even without a damper.

This picture clearly shows the independent rear suspension setup on Graham Shaw's Bandit trike. The differential is mounted inside a cradle, similar to the Casarva setup. Unequal length wishbones are linked to coilover shocks to provide a more stable ride over uneven surfaces. This suspension system is quite common on kit cars. Note the chain drive rear axle, a feature found on most quad bikes. This one uses a Ford Sierra limited slip diff with the differential housing, machined to install the sprocket on the left-hand face of the flange. This trike also has a tow-bar fitted; a useful feature, as many trikers use their machines to haul small trailers on tours. Axe Customs is based in Nottinghamshire, UK, and produces billet parts, as well as carrying out custom work and fabrication.

production trikes

Can-Am Spyder/Bombardier Recreational Products

In 2007, Snowmobile and watercraft maker Bombardier Recreational Products introduced its first 'on-road' vehicle, a 'reverse' trike known as the Can-Am Spyder TM Roadster.

Bombardier Recreational Products (BRP) still produces snowmobiles and watercraft, as well as outboard motors and ATVs. BRP also enjoys a good business relationship with Rotax, the Austrian engine manufacturer. Rotax supplies engines for most of BRP's vehicles.

The Can-Am Spyder first appeared in 2007. This Canadian company began by producing snowmobiles and off-road vehicles, and now builds these reverse trikes at its Valcourt, Quebec headquarters. Powered by a 990cc Rotax V-twin engine delivering 106bhp (78kW), the Spyder is aimed at the touring market. Riders are given the option of a five-speed manual or electronic sequential gearbox. Reverse gear comes as standard, and is a true mechanical version, rather than an electric option found on most trikes. Shown here is the aggressively styled RS Sport, with matt black paintwork and recessed headlamps. The front steering assembly is similar to that of a car, with coilover shock absorbers and wishbone, independent front suspension. The Spyder also has power-assisted steering. There are various technological features built into the Spyder to help the rider stay on track. The stability control system (SCS) calculates the vehicle's appropriate response via feedback from the handlebars. The system individually brakes the wheels, and regulates the engine torque, until the rider regains control. Spyders also have ABS anti-lock brakes and traction control.

The Spyder also has a useful 58-litre (2.05ft³) of luggage space in the front compartment.

Matthew Bullock (left) and jet ski champion James Bushell run 158 Performance, selling Can-Am Spyders and other Bombardier Recreational Products, such as quad bikes and jet-skis. The Spyder shown here is the RT model, with different headlamp design. RT stands for Road Touring, as opposed to the RS model, which stands for Road Sports, hence its more aggressive look. The RT comes equipped with full-colour instrument display, giving information on speed, time, temperature, and distance, plus an AM/FM radio with iPod adaptor. Further creature comforts include heated rider and passenger hand grips, cruise control, satellite navigation, and electric height adjustment for the windscreen.

The Spyder looks striking from any angle. The wide front track of 1384mm (54.5in) provides good roadholding characteristics. Overall width is 1582mm (62.3in).

Can-Am Spyder front suspension detail. This machine has an electronically-controlled power steering system. The independent front suspension soaks up uneven road surfaces, well assisted by twin gas-charged shock absorbers. Bump steer – the tendency for the handlebars to steer as the suspension jerks upward – is not a problem for the Spyder.

The Spyder RT is a little more laidback than the RS, and is marketed as a rival to the various three-wheeled Goldwing and Harley trikes. The bodykit on this trike allows 155 litres of storage space. Plush seats provide good lumbar support. Passenger armrests provide additional support, should the pillion fall asleep on a long journey.

Rewaco trike from Germany shown here, with top box fitted, plus a few personal touches.

Rewaco

Rewaco Spezialfahrzeuge GmbH has been producing trikes at its factory in Lindlar, near Cologne,Germany, since 1990. Rewaco points out that all of its trikes meet the European registration standards e1*2002/24, and are street legal in all EC member states, as well as the USA, Canada, Japan, and Australia. Many Rewaco trike owners are non-motorcyclists, so take advantage of the fact the trikes can, like most trikes, be ridden/driven with a car licence. There is also a thriving owners club, where enthusiasts can go on ride-outs together, and be informed of triking events. Most Rewaco trikes have a long wheelbase, and the driver sits very low in the frame, with feet forward. The passenger sits much higher, looking over the driver's head. Behind the passenger is the engine, mounted between the two wide rear wheels. In some models, the engine is hidden inside the compartment, covered by the vast bulbous rear bodywork, and faired-in rear mudguards. However, Rewaco has more recently been working on bike conversions, too. The Suzuki CT 800, CT 1500S, and CT 1800S bikes have proved worthy donors for very stylish-looking trikes.

Ford-engined Rewaco trike pictured at a bike show in East Anglia, UK. Plenty of room for three to travel in style. A few entrepreneurs offer trike tours in various countries around the world. The rider/driver acts as chauffeur, while the two rear passengers sit back and enjoy the scenery.

Detail showing the car type gearlever mounted on the fuel tank. Note also the twin speakers.

The Ford Zetec engine sits neatly inside the rear compartment on this Rewaco. The engine is a 1596cc unit, producing 115bhp (85kW) in normally-aspirated form, and 140bhp (103kW) in GTS turbo versions. The GTR engine produces an eye-watering 185bhp (136kW).

The RevTech air-cooled V-twin engine is very similar to the Harley-Davidson engine.
The unit in this Rewaco trike is mounted to an adaptor plate, manufactured by Rewaco.
It is coupled to a Volkswagen Beetle gearbox, driveshaft, and hubs.

According to Rewaco sales literature, the Suzuki Intruder is the perfect base for converting a bike to a trike. Judging by the style and finish of this machine, we can easily see why. Trike models are CT 800S, CT 1500S, and CT 1800S.

This Boom trike uses the Volkswagen flat-four air-cooled Beetle engine as its power source. With capacities ranging from 1200cc up to 1800cc, it is a popular choice for trike builders. It is very similar in concept to the Rewaco. Both manufacturers started out together in Germany before going their separate ways. Rewaco and Boom build complete trikes from scratch. They also convert motorcycles to trikes, which are then sold to the customer. This trike is definitely built to attract attention. The soundtrack from those vertical stack twin exhausts is bound to get the neighbours' curtains twitching. Triking can be a social affair, as this machine is a three-seater. One can imagine conversation to be difficult at speed, however.

Boom Trikes

Boom Trikes Fahrzeugbau GmbH is situated in Sontheim an der Brenz. The first trike was called the Highway Series 1, and was fitted with wide wheels and a tuned Volkswagen Beetle engine mounted at the rear. Company founders, Wolfgang Merkle and Hermann Böhm, tested the Highway I on the Hockenheim racetrack. In 1992, the Highway Series II made its debut at the IAA motor show in Frankfurt. Sales of the trike did well, and by August 1998, Boom Trikes received EU technical approval. The following year saw a real breakthrough at international level, and in 2000, these machines were tested under extreme conditions in Morocco. Boom Trikes

has fitted both motorcycle and car engines in its trikes. The Boom V2 uses a 800cc V-twin engine, with CVT automatic transmission. At the other end of the range is the Mustang ST1 Trike, which is fitted with a Ford Zetec 1.6 water-cooled car engine. In Europe, Boom Trikes offers a smaller version called the V1, which has a 500cc single-cylinder engine. The trikes are built using vehicle construction techniques, from traditional steel or aluminium frames. Engines are sourced from Piaggio, Ford, Peugeot, and VW-Mexico. All axles, frames, forks, wiring harnesses, and bespoke parts are produced in-house by Boom. Bodywork is manufactured and painted locally. Other components, such as brakes, electrical equipment, and tyres are sourced from leading

European automotive suppliers. Many of the trikes feature waterproof and removable top boxes, aluminium chassis and wheels, wide tyres, front and rear disc brakes, handbrake, extensive use of stainless steel, and a patented front fork. Boom Trikes have become Europe's leading trike maker in 2007. Since then, every second trike sold in Europe is a Boom. There are over 9000 Boom Trikes on the road. It is interesting to note that the founders of Rewaco, Boom, and two others, namely WK Trikes and Fitch, all worked together in a barn in the early days. All these trikes are very similar in design.

This Boom trike resembles a wild animal rising on its haunches and waiting to pounce. Rear passengers have an elevated position, and the 'pilot' sits low to the ground. Chrome tubing offers side impact protection, and deters the rider from putting his feet down.

The sting in this Boom trike's tail is a 1.6-litre Ford Zetec car engine. Power output is 110bhp (84kW), and can achieve 108.7mph (175km/h).

Piaggio MP3

The Piaggio factory is based in Pontedera, Italy. Founded by Rinaldo Piaggio in 1884, Piaggio initially produced locomotives and railway carriages. However, Piaggio is famously known for its iconic Vespa scooters, which the company has been producing since the 1940s. Despite producing the most successful scooter of all time, in 2004, Piaggio was in a financial crisis. Stiff competition from the Japanese was a major threat to sales. The company then rolled out a gas-electric hybrid scooter, and a sophisticated tilting scooter, with two wheels in front and one in back to grip the road better. However, unlike most three-wheelers, it leaned around corners, thus handling more like a conventional two-wheeler. An alloy parallelogram front suspension setup enabled the machine to lean, and also for each front wheel to move up and down independently. 125cc, 300cc, and 400cc versions are currently available. A 250cc version was available until recently, but has been superseded by the 300cc. Gilera, which is now owned by Piaggio, produces a sporty, aggressively-styled version of the MP3, called the Fuoco 500. The 125cc version is not available in the US, and the Fuoco is sold as the MP3 500. June 2009 saw the advent of the MP3 400 LT, which,

The MP3 was introduced in 2004 and was a stylish looking scooter with two front wheels. An innovation for Piaggio, it attracted favourable attention from the press. The MP3 has appeared with various engine sizes, namely 125cc, 250cc, 300cc, and 400cc. Production of the 250cc has now ceased, and is replaced by the 300. A version of the MP3, called the LT, has been produced to exploit a loophole in the law. Most MP3s are too narrow to be classed as trikes, but the LT has a lengthened track – hence the letters 'LT' – and is therefore registered as a trike. To qualify for trike status, the front track, or distance between the front wheels, needs to be 465mm apart. The standard front-end width is 420mm.This opens up the opportunity for those who only possess a full car driving licence, especially affluent European city dwellers looking for transport suitable for an urban environment. The MP3 is the most expensive scooter in its class, which is enough to deter car drivers, who could buy a small hatchback for the same money. However, the MP3 offers excellent safety, with stopping distances 20 per cent shorter than conventional scooters. The two front wheels allow for sure-footed handling, especially on slippery surfaces, where a conventional two-wheeler might 'break away' at the front. The MP3 uses the Piaggio leader 125cc engine – a single-cylinder four-stroke, four-valve, liquid-cooled 15bhp (11kw) with CVT automatic transmission.

having a slightly wider track and a few other minor modifications, made it legal to ride with a car licence. Piaggio introduced a hybrid version to the range, with a plug-in charging system. The 3.5hp (2.6kW) electric motor can be used as power assistance for the 125cc petrol engine, or can be used on its own. However, on its own, it has a limited range of 11 miles (18km), and can manage a top speed of only 20mph (32km/h). With both power units used simultaneously, the machine is a willing performer, with 0-60mph (0-97 km/h) attainable in 5 seconds. Fuel economy is an abstemious 169mpg (141 mpg US) and 1.67 litres per 100km. Unfortunately, riders can only enjoy these benefits for 25 minutes at a time, until the batteries go flat, and then have to rely on the 125cc engine to power the 249kg (550lb) scooter. MP3 is an acronym, standing for Moto Piaggio a 3 ruote. In other words, a Piaggio motorcycle with three wheels!

The Piaggio MP3 LT has a front track of 465mm, which means it is classed as a trike, not a motorcycle, in most European countries. However, due to its ability to lean, it handles like a normal scooter.

The Gilera Fuoco has a 500cc single-cylinder liquid-cooled engine with CVT transmission. In the US, it is badged as the MP3 500. It is more aggressively styled than its Piaggio sibling, but its underpinnings are the same.

Xingyue Vogue

Xingyue produces around 1.1 million motorcycles annually, a reflection of the rise of Chinese manufacturing generally. Inspired by the Honda Gyro, the Xingyue Vogue is a comparatively rare sight in Europe and the US, where imports trickle in, but is popular in its native country and Japan. A remarkable feature of the Xingyue is the canopy, which affords some protection from the elements.

The Xingyue Vogue is marketed under different names in various countries around the world. It is also known as the Palmo 150, MotoMojo Tri-Elite, Scooter Pod, Orbitor, Tri-Fecta, Manhattan 3, and Automoto. It is an entirely different animal to most of the trikes featured here, but deserves a mention as a motorcycle-based trike.

Designed mainly for commuting and town use, the Xingyue Vogue offers unrivalled weather protection, and enough storage space to swallow a full-face helmet and some shopping. It even has its own windscreen wiper. It uses the same principle as the original Ariel Three and the Honda Gyro, with a tilting canopy hingeing above a separate rear drive unit, which remains level. Headroom is limited for tall riders wearing helmets, and the sturdy windscreen pillars do obstruct the view somewhat.

The 150cc four stroke engine is fan-cooled, and drives the two rear wheels via a fully enclosed gear-driven differential. The engine is a Chinese copy of the Honda GY6 single cylinder unit, producing a modest 7.5bhp. (5.6kW). In terms of performance, this scooter trike will just about manage 50mph (80km/h). This scooter might feel odd to the uninitiated, rather like a two-wheeler towing a small trailer, due to the two rear wheels carrying the mass of engine and transmission. However, with a little practice, the Vogue will lean like a normal scooter. With the two wheels at the back, it should be less susceptible to skidding on slippery surfaces. Below the engine, the tilting mechanism can be seen, attached to the crankcase by a bracket. The other end is bolted to the shock absorber, just visible in the picture.

Bill Hill, of Commuter Concepts, demonstrates the leaning capability of the Xingyue Vogue. It also has a cable-operated mechanical tilt lock system to safeguard against falling over when parked. Fuel consumption is around 80-100mpg UK or 67-83mpg US (3.5 litres per 100km to 2.8 litres per 100km).

It is worth looking at different ends of the triking spectrum, and this little scooter trike serves as a contrast to the kind of mass-produced machines available. Made in Shandong, China, this is a Pioneer XF 150 ZK, which has been imported to the UK by LIA Imports. Pioneer is a subsidiary of the Jinan Qingqi Group. Originally founded in 1956, Jinan Qingqi produces mopeds, quadbikes, and other small-engined and electric motorcycles. Unlike the Xingyue Vogue, the Pioneer doesn't lean round corners, but does boast a reverse gear. There is also a 125cc version. Power output is similar to the Vogue, as the Pioneer uses a similar Honda copy Chinese engine. This machine has a narrow track for a non-leaning trike. It can fit through the average doorway, but handling could be tricky, especially at speed. Transmission is automatic CVT, with a secondary chain driving the two rear wheels via a differential.

This is a Jinlun scooter trike made by the Zhejiang Wanjin Industry Co Ltd, in Yongkang, China. It is somewhat larger than the Jinan Qingqi Pioneer Trike. It has quite sleek styling, with a comfortable, wide, low seat. This trike has a wider rear track than the Pioneer, so although it's not as agile in traffic, handling should be less skittish. A GY6 type 200cc single-cylinder four-stroke engine with Constantly Variable Transmission (CVT) provides the power. A V-belt drives a clutch coupling, which is then connected to a chain. The chain then drives the two rear wheels by a quad bike-type differential. The engine produces 14.8bhp (11kW) at 7500rpm.

homemade trikes

This short wheelbase trike has been adapted for its disabled rider.

Note the chain-driven differential and rear tow-bar. Judging by the sticker, this trike's owner seems to have a positive attitude, and doesn't let a disability get in the way.

This unique trike clearly demonstrates the extreme end of the trike spectrum. The one-fingered salute serves as a gesture of defiance to conformity. The handlebars turn the front wheel remotely by a linkage. The front forks appear to have been forged during the Industrial Revolution, and the rest of the trike is mounted on a solid frame. With its rear bench seat and open-top configuration, this trike probably feels like a vintage touring car. However, that Ford V6 engine up front ensures this machine is no slouch.

There is a lot of scope for the home trike builder, in terms of different designs. Trikes can be made to suit any budget, and can be any size. However, for licencing laws, a trike must fall within a certain weight limit. In the UK, this is 550kg, although the 'class 3' MoT (Ministry of Transport) test weight limit is 450kg or under. (For those outside the UK, the 'MoT' is an annual roadworthiness test for motor vehicles.) Heavier trikes, by law, would therefore be classed as cars, and would be subject to different testing. Some trikes are built as workhorses. Costing little to build, they won't win any prizes, but are solid, reliable, and capable of regular use. Then there are the show trikes. With bright colour schemes, masses of chrome, and loud engines, they are built purely to attract attention. There are numerous clubs which exist to support

the triking world. Many of these trike and motorcycle clubs raise money for charity, and promote lots of worthy causes. Coffin Scratchers MCC supports Heartlink and also Glenfield Children's Hospital in the UK. Every year, the club organises three rallies and two shows. It's a family-orientated club, whose president is one Alan Cayliss, as mentioned elsewhere in this book.

There are numerous clubs throughout the world a triking enthusiast can join. Probably the largest is Brothers of the Third Wheel. It was established in 1983 by Jim Sickler in the US. As a global phenomenon, its aim is to unite trikers everywhere, and to provide advice on trikes and triking. With 6000 members worldwide, everyone is encouraged to attend rallies and join in the fun. Obviously, the level of participation is down to the individual.

Most trikers personalise their machines in some way. The rats adorning this trike enhance its already rugged appearance. Perhaps their snarling expressions help to ward off intruders.

Simon Farrier, seen here on the right, with fellow triker Pete Collins, built this machine himself in 1995. He used a Reliant chassis and plenty of scaffold pipe! The vehicle's V5 log book documentation has it listed as a 'Reliant Trike.' The trike's front end is from a 750 Honda. Simon has had a lot of use out of his machine, which served as everyday transport for a while. The rear carrier has a fold-down seat, and is also used to haul stones and tools for his job as a dry stone wall builder. Simon sold it previously, but realised he missed its usefulness, so bought it back. He claims it was cheap to make, and is very strong. The British Reliant Robin and Rialto three-wheeled cars are a popular basis for a trike conversion because they lend themselves so well to this application. The Reliant engine has a fairly low power output compared to most bike engines of a similar capacity, but is a straightforward, reliable unit, free-revving and lightweight. With its gearbox, it enjoys the bonus of reverse gear. The Reliant chassis also yields a useful back axle.

A motorcycle accident prompted Phil Waiton to consider trikes, and eventually led him to an abandoned project. He picked up 'Ultimate Warrior' in Scotland in 2009, getting stuck in snow on the way there. Ultimate Warrior is powered by a Nissan Micra 1350cc car engine, with automatic gearbox. The engine is fitted behind the front seat and is mounted to a subframe, using many of the original Nissan parts. It is enclosed in a glassfibre cover, which hinges from the back to allow excellent access. Phil claims the trike has brilliant performance, and is capable of 100mph. He also says it is very easy to ride. Phil plans to modify the rear cover so he can fit a passenger seat, thus making the whole experience a more social occasion.

This picture clearly shows how easily accessible the engine is, by simply lifting the rear cover. The Nissan engine is no fire-breathing powerhouse, but has the benefit of Japanese-car reliability and good fuel economy. In such a lightweight vehicle, it would be no slouch, either. Using the whole engine and transmission from a front-wheel drive car, and grafting a motorcycle front end to it, is a simple solution and one used by upmarket trikes such as Boom and Rewaco. This trike is perfectly capable of regular use and long journeys – weather permitting. It also has the advantage of Nissan spares back-up.

Owner Grum built this trike, his first attempt, but it took him seven years. He'd build another, too, if given the chance. Grum didn't use jigs to line up everything during the build. When he started, the trike was laid out on blocks of wood, and free-formed around that. To save costs, Grum used offcuts from a fabrication shop. The engine is from a MkII Escort Mexico 1600. He just happened to have it lying around, and it was originally destined for a kit car. The gearbox is from a MkII Escort 1300. The rear axle started its life in a three-litre Ford Capri, but has since been shortened by two inches (4.8mm) on the nearside. The front end came from a 750 Kawasaki, donated by a friend (it had been run over by a truck). The handbrake is a Ford Escort MkIV item. Grum's trike had to undergo the British SVA test (applies to all homebuilt road vehicles) before being declared roadworthy. "Make sure you have receipts for everything, including all materials used," he says.

Rat owns this 2.3-litre V6 diesel-engined trike. The engine originally came from an American taxi. It took six months to build this large machine, which has a Yamaha 1100 front end, a Ford Granada rear axle, and an automatic gearbox. The fuel tank consists of two regular motorcycle tanks linked together by a pipe. Rat reckons his trike will do 120mph and 33mpg – although not at the same time. This trike gets used regularly, and has been on trips to the south coast in the UK.

This rear-engined Volkswagen trike was started in 1999, and finished a year later, just before the new UK Single Vehicle Approval (SVA) test was introduced. Owner Skunk was able to retain the original registration number. The engine is a 1300cc twin port, producing around 49bhp. The wide wheels came from a Suzuki Vitara Jeep. Built from scratch, this trike uses a box section chassis, and a Honda 400 front end. The fuel tank is likely to have come from a Suzuki Intruder, although Skunk isn't completely certain. His skills as a CNC engineer have definitely helped in the building. This trike is the sole means of transport for single parent Skunk and his two kids. Not only does he use it for shopping, he has taken this machine across France, from Normandy down to the south, and on to the Italian border.

Ged Kettle acquired his trike in 2006. Since then, he has been all over Germany, Belgium, and Holland. He hopes to take it to Cyprus in the near future. It gets used nearly every day, and all year round, so Ged is obviously a seasoned triker. His wife also rides the trike. Despite its size, the Nissan 2.7-litre diesel engine ensures rapid and frugal progress. A Ford Granada rear axle divides all that power equally between the two rear wheels. The registration document lists the trike as 'Bell 1,' was designed by a Jeff Bell, and built by Trike Design.

This trike belongs to enthusiast Foggy, in Huddersfield, UK. This is more or less how the trike looked when Foggy acquired it. This is another example of the popular Volkswagen engine choice. Most of the VW components can be used, so it's a case of skilfully mating car and bike together. Since the photo was taken, this trike has had a full rebuild, new body kit, wiring, and paint job. It was first built in 2002, and rebuilt six years later. It has since been fitted with a new 1600cc engine. (Courtesy Foggy)

Geordie hasn't owned his Reliant trike for long, but finds it fun to ride, and it attracts attention wherever it goes.

The Leper was built as a one-off by its previous owner, and has had a few personal touches added since. Joe 90 of the Eagles Motorcycle Club bought the trike in 2008. Power comes from a rear-mounted Skoda 1300cc engine, and a Honda Superdream front-end completes the picture. The trike is used mainly for bike and trike meetings, including Goth rallies at Whitby, north Yorkshire, UK, where money is raised for charity. Make no bones about it, this trike's quota of skulls and wildlife effigies give it a brooding, malevolent presence.

Pete Collins is Area Captain of the Brothers of the Third Wheel, Derbyshire Chapter. His trike is a Reliant-based hardtail. Built in 1997, it is registered as 'Dolphin' trike, and has been in Pete's possession since 2002. He uses it every week for pleasure and riding to rallies. He has also ridden to Belgium.

This home-built trike uses a pressed-steel box frame, and is fitted with a highly tuned Skoda engine. Rear wheels are driven through the Skoda transaxle; a similar layout to that of the Volkswagen.

A 3.5-litre Rover V8 car engine propels this home-built special to breakneck speeds.

Detail showing Rover V8 engine installation. Car engine mounts are neatly grafted on to a tubular bike frame.

Arguably more car than trike, this one-off is powered by a Kawasaki 650cc engine.

This Kawasaki-based trike employs a simple effective design, with some additional bracing between the solid rear axle and the swing arm.

The Ford Pinto engine and the steering linkage to remote handlebars are prominent features of this trike.

Photgraphed at the UK National Exhibition Centre in 2009, this custom trike is truly a work of art.

chapter 5

conclusion

Triking covers such a broad spectrum, with numerous machines of different sizes and layouts. Triking is a very individual means of transport that, conversely, has a huge following. The possibilities for trike builders are endless, and these pages show that the machines don't have to be high-tech or high budget. For many, it's a means of escape. Whether it's a blast down the motorway coming home from work, or a grand tour across America, triking for many provides a welcome diversion from the humdrum routine of daily life. Trike builders face engineering challenges, and often finish up with something truly unique. That is what makes them so appealing. As long as enthusiasts embrace these challenges, this niche form of motoring will have a following for many years to come.

I want to be a Harley when I grow up.

Also from Veloce –

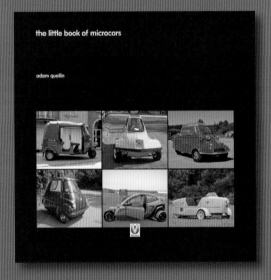

the little book of microcars

adam quellin

ISBN: 978-1-845842-78-9
Paperback • 14x14cm • £4.99* UK/$9.95* USA • 96 pages • 85 colour and b&w pictures

During the middle of the twentieth century, a plethora of small economy cars – often quirky and bizarre – emerged to meet the needs of the cash-strapped motorist. This book charts the history and development of these microcars, from the lean period after the Second World War right up to the present day.

For more info on Veloce titles, visit our website at www.veloce.co.uk
• email: info@veloce.co.uk • Tel: +44(0)1305 260068 * prices subject to change, p&p extra

index